LENA

life story of my mother

by sis laraux

Lena, Life Story of My Mother

ISBN: 0-9644809-1-3

© 2002 by Sis Laraux
First Edition

Manufactured in Anchorage, Alaska
Printed & Designed By A.T. Publishing & Printing

All rights reserved, including the right of reproduction in any form, or by any mechanical or electronic means including photocopying or recording, or by any information storage or retrieval system, in whole or in part in any form, and in any case not without the written permission of the author and publisher.

DEDICATION

Camai, "greetings"

This book is dedicated to the memory of my parents,
Arthur and Lena Laraux.

To my brothers and sister who have passed on, Alfred
(Butch), Arthur Jr. (Sonny), Amel, and Ruby.

To those still living, Hanna, Bess, Lena, and Charlie

Also to my niece Zoanne Gregory Anderson
for her help in writing this book about Mom

TABLE OF CONTENTS

Lena 1

Cleanliness 5

Anguss 9

Mom's Hunting 11

Diseases 15

Clothes 19

Fishing 25

Green Thumb 29

Eskimo Dances 31

Christmas 33

Games 35

Laplanders .31

Burbot or Lush 41

The War 43

Later Years .47

The Lord's Prayer 57

LENA life story of my mother

Our maternal great-grandmother was born on Nelson Island off of the coast of Alaska, before Alaska was bought from Russia. Her Yup'ik Eskimo name was Kwimiak. She did not have an English name. Along the coast of Alaska where the Russians landed and did their trading of guns, they left their mark; Kwimiak had light-colored eyes, hair, and complexion, although we could not determine just how much Russian she was.

When she was in her teens, Kwimiak moved to the mainland of Alaska with her parents. They traveled in a large, hand-sewn walrus skin boat with all their belongings. On this trip she gave birth to my grandmother Anna, right in the middle of the Bering Sea. We called Anna by her Eskimo name, Annun. The family settled at the mouth of the Kuskokwim River in a village called Nunachak. It was close to Nunapitchuk and Kasigluk, and is now deserted.

As the years went by, Grandma Annun lived with Wasillie Shepherd in a common-law marriage. She gave birth to three children—my mother, Lena, my aunt Bessie, and a son who died as a baby. My mother was born on August 12, 1902. Her Eskimo name was "Uryuralria", which means "overflows".

2 LENA life story of my mother

When Mom and Bessie were in their teens, Annun moved upriver to Bethel and then to Akiak, where the first government hospital was built on the other side of the river. The hospital had a light plant for electricity, which the village also used. Grandma met miner Joseph Venes and married him, settling at Old Akiak as it is called now. A small trading post was built, and miners and Laplanders settled there. Annun and Joe had three more children, Nora, Joe Jr., and Elias. Wasillie Shepherd married later also and had two daughters, Carrie and Eileen. Mom worked as a housekeeper for the trader Carl I. Carlson and his wife Wenke, until my father, Arthur Laraux (formerly L'Heureux) came to Akiak to live with his mining friend Wilfred Reno. Arthur and Wilfred came to Alaska in the Dawson gold rush days in 1898 and then went on to the gold stampede at Iditarod, Alaska, before coming down the Kuskokwim to settle and build homes at Akiak.

Grandma Venes - Annun, Great Grandma - Kwimiak, Mother Lena - Uryuralria, Baby Lena - Cutie

Mother was a very tiny person, standing 4' 6" in her adulthood and weighing right around eighty-five pounds. She spoke in broken English, which embarrassed her, however she was very witty and humorous. She had many expressions of her own that were clever and hilarious.

My father married my mother in 1922 and Wilfred married her sister Bessie. Both partners were French Canadians from Quebec, Canada. They built homes and raised foxes, mink, and pigs. They bought horses from another miner that was moving to Bristol Bay, and had a regular farm going with gardens and oat fields. The oats were for the horses. There were two of them until one got sick and died. Papa had built a barn where the horses and oat supply were kept. I remember the horses were used for tilling gardens for people in the village. They also came in handy for moving buildings and

Akiak Territorial School 1940.

Charles - adopted as a baby - half brother of Ruby - Airplane Pilot.

Arthur and Lena Laraux. Mom holding Emil, Hanna, Rosanna, Arthur Jr, Bess, Lena & Alfred.

hauling wood from the wood camp outside of Akiak, where it was cut.

Wood was hauled by bobsled to a small sawmill my father had. It was cut and used as fuel for the local homes. It was also sold to the sternwheelers that freighted up and down the river, for energy to power the boats. My grandfather Joe Venes built a one-room territorial school in the middle of the village, where we all attended grade school. It was also wood-heated.

There were seven of us children, Hanna, Arthur Jr. (Sonny), myself named Rosanna (everyone calls me Sis), Alfred (Butch), Bess, Lena, (whom we call Cutie, pronounced "Cootie"), and Amel. The four oldest were all born at the small two-story hospital across on the other side of the river. Bessie, Lena and Amel were delivered at home with the help of our Grandmother Annun. We never seemed to pay much attention to expectant mothers, as we figured it was a natural thing. Sometimes we'd be playing ball or other outdoor games, and would come home to a new sister or brother that my grandmother had helped deliver. It was so exciting!

Papa had a kind, gentle temperament and never touched us to spank or discipline. Mom always said, "Your Papa was the nicest man I ever meet whole my life."

In later years, our father sold his fox and mink farm and went back to mining. He also worked on the mine freighter with a Japanese man named Tony Sumi. Tony's boat was called the MINK. Papa was the engineer, and they hauled freight for the mine, from Bethel to the Tuluksak River to the Lower Landing where the mine sent tractors to haul freight. The mine was close to the Alaska Range.

Ruby Reno - Raised along with us after her mother passed away.

Middy Chaney and Butch Laraux with Mom's first grandchild, Harvey Johnson.

CLEANLINESS

Mom was obsessed with health and cleanliness, due to the diseases on the other side of Akiak in the Eskimo village, and at the hospital. There were so many people with tuberculosis and other contagious diseases. People were dying and since there were so many of us, Mom was afraid we'd contract something. Clorox was the best disinfectant and it seemed we used so much of it for cleaning.

When visitors from the villages would come, "camai"s were said, the Eskimo greeting word (pronounced "chu-MY"). We made plenty of tea, and served pilot bread (large, round crackers), dried fish, salmon, and akutaq. The akutaq was made with tundra berries of all kinds, including cranberries, blueberries and salmonberries, mixed with Crisco or Wesson oil and sugar. Sometimes we added in fresh snow to make it creamier. It is a great Alaska treat. There would be lots of Eskimo conversation, and then they would finally leave with plenty of quyanas, ("quee-ON-uh"), meaning "thank you". We'd have to gather up all the dishes that were used, and sterilize them by boiling them in Clorox water. It's a good thing we had heavy-duty dishes to take the treatment.

6 LENA life story of my mother

Saturday was a work day for us. All had duties to perform, the girls inside and the boys outside with Papa, after having a good breakfast of sourdough hotcakes, bacon, and eggs if we had enough. We had dried eggs but we only baked with those. We also had homemade syrup with breakfast. Complete housework was done, scrubbing floors and moving furniture around to get under it, dusting the homemade furniture that our father had made in his own shop. Even today we can see some of the furniture that he made in the homes of our family that still lives in Bethel. Beds had to be changed and made, rugs shaken, just like k.p. in the army. Oh, and don't forget emptying the chamber pots! None of us liked that job but it had to be done, otherwise we'd have to run to the outhouse in the middle of the night.

The boys hauled river water for cleaning and washing. They had a small sled with a barrel and bucket, and a few dogs to help haul up and down the hill, filling galvanized water barrels. Wood had to be sawed and cut for the furnace and kitchen stove. We had a basement furnace that heated the house, so a chute was built to furnish the basement stove. The basement was used for vegetables and other cold storage items.

Joe Chaney, a miner left with five motherless boys, lived at Akiak. He would spend a lot of time with our family. All the boys were sent to the Holy Cross mission and as they each got old enough to work he had them come home for him to raise after the territorial school was built on our side of the river. Our brothers were close friends, and one boy named Amidee (we called him Middy) became one of the family. He stayed right with us and worked, and was so helpful with everything. He stayed with our family until the second world war broke out. Then he went off to serve his country.

Middy, the boys, and Papa would hitch up the dogs or harness Barney, the horse, and go to the woodcamp to cut wood. They would haul the wood back and saw the pieces up for firewood or for building. They sold to the sternwheeler or anyone that needed wood for heat.

An ice house was built. The men of the village would cut ice from the river and store it with sawdust for drinking water, and we had enough to make ice cream when we wanted it.

In the early spring, the coast boats with their Eskimo captains and crew would arrive, bringing their seals, seal oil and walrus from the Kuskokwim Bay. In our excitement, we would yell to each other, "The seal boats are here!" They would trade for clothing, groceries or cash from the gussuk (white) traders. The gussuks would buy the seal and walrus products to trade later with the local natives. I believe the word "gussuk" came from the Russian word, "Cossack."

Carl I. Carlson, the Akiak store owner, had a large water pit dug and built behind a warehouse, where he stored whole seal pokes filled with seal oil. The seal pokes were the entire seal skin with the hair removed. Seal oil is a delicacy eaten over meat, fish, or mixed with akutaq. Our family never got accustomed to it but when Mom and her Eskimo friends got together we just closed the doors and went somewhere else. The smell was so potent, and the older the oil got, the stronger it smelled. When the kids got to rough housing with each other, someone would threaten to throw them in Carl I. Carlson's seal hole!

We grew up with no vitamins except for a tablespoon of cod liver oil daily. It was very hard to take even if we tried to diguise it with juice. It reminded us too much of the smell of seal oil! It did keep us pretty healthy, though.

8 LENA life story of my mother

Mom and Bessie in the spring of 1932.

ANGUSS

When we were small and still unable to be much help to Mother, we sometimes had one of Mom's friends or a girl of working age come from the other side of the river to help with the washing, ironing, and babies. Diaper washing was done over the wash board, and then they were hung outside on the clotheslines to dry. In the winter, the diapers and lightweight clothing were hung on the clotheslines that crossed the children's large bedroom. The pants and heavier clothes were hung out to "freeze-dry" outdoors, and after being frozen they'd be brought in to finish drying on the line in the house. Sometimes a relative would come from a village and stay awhile and help mother with all these chores. The helpers would be paid in food or clothing that they or their families needed, and they were so glad to have it.

One of our house girls was an Eskimo girl from Nunapitchuk, a village below Bethel. We called her by her Eskimo name, Anguss (pronounced "Ung-oosh"). I never knew her English name. She spent quite a few years living with us. We were all young, and I got very attached to Anguss since I was the youngest then, about three or four years old. I spent a lot of time with her. She was such a big help for Mother and became like a family member. She was a lot of fun. The Chaney boys that were always around teased her a lot, and so did the village kids. I remember one afternoon while we were on the back porch, some teenage boys came laughing and running around the house, hauling the little Laplander, Ole Polk. They grabbed Anguss, put her on a chair, and made Ole sit on her lap and forced them to kiss. It was a big commotion with Anguss shouting and me crying for Mom to come. Out the door Mom flew with a broom in her hand after the boys in their mischief. The broom seemed to be one of her favorite weapons for everything,

Pappa, baby Sis, Momma, Hanna and Sonny in 1927.

including wandering dogs. All the boys got swatted good but ran away laughing. There was always something to have a good laugh about. Early one spring a boat came to Akiak to get Anguss to go back home. In those days, marriages were planned by the older folks of the village, so she had to leave to get married. I was crying my heart out, rolling in the fresh dirt of the newly planted potato garden. No one could console me. The memory remains strong in my mind. I never saw Anguss again. About a year after she went home and got married, news came that she had passed away.

MOM'S HUNTING

Our father didn't do much hunting but would go out to the reindeer camp and get reindeer from the Laplanders. In those days, the price for a carcass was ten dollars. He'd come home with our dogteam and a sled all loaded with reindeer meat. He'd hang it in the wood shed and it looked like a slaughter house in there. It hung until warm weather came and then we would all get busy cutting and canning and salting meat. It was Mother that did all the hunting of game and she taught us all how to hunt.

Mom would dress up with a parkie, mittens, and mukluks. The mukluks were made of reindeer hide and wolf, and went up to her hips. She would take her lunch and twenty-two rifle and a single-shot shotgun. Off she'd go with three dogs and a sled. I can't ever remember her coming home with an empty sled. She'd have rabbits, ptarmigan, and in early spring, geese, muskrats or ducks. Since we didn't have beef, all this was so good besides the reindeer. When she'd go muskrat hunting, she'd also clean and skin the pelt for sale to the local store or the fur buyer that came to the village.

12 LENA life story of my mother

Early one spring, my oldest sister Hanna and I decided to go hunting geese and ducks. In those days it wasn't legal, but we always went anyway when the birds came. At the sand bar where a bunch of them were eating we were sneaking up on them on our hands and knees. She was ahead of me. I had a twenty-two rifle. All of a sudden the gun went off and the bullet lodged right between Hanna's legs. Oh, what a scare we had! The birds all lit off into the sky, and we were so upset, we decided to go home. We didn't tell the folks, as we knew they'd restrict us from hunting. Quite a while later we told them about the near-accident, and we got a talk on gun safety and use of the gun lock.

Mom setting out for a days hunt with a 3 dog team.

When we got birds, we'd have to pluck the feathers out in the woods, saving them for pillows or whatever they were used for. Someone would always be watching out for the game warden to fly over when he made his rounds of the villages.

Mom would take each one of us out to teach us how to snare ptarmigan and rabbits. Using the same twine that salmon nets were made of, she would pick a spot in small willows, where lots of ptarmigan would land and eat the willows. Making a willow fence about twelve feet long, Mom would leave an open space at one-foot intervals, large enough for a bird to get through. She'd place a round twine snare there, securing the snare tightly to the willow fencing. Then when the bird would try to go through the opening, it would get caught in the twine. She got a lot of birds that way. The rabbit snares were made in the same manner, usually on a permanent rabbit trail under a tree that had fallen over. All this game would add variety to our usual diet.

Mother was such a good cook. We would get some corned beef, canned ham, bacon, and Spam, sent by steamship from Seattle in early spring and late fall before freezeup. But when she got ptarmigan, rabbits, geese, or ducks, she would fix them in such delicious ways. She'd braise the birds like chicken, and have lots of good onion gravy and garlic mashed potatoes, with garden vegetables on the side, and was dinner ever good! Of course, we'd have akutaq, Eskimo ice cream. We'd come home from school or playing outside to fresh bread, or assaliaq which was fried bread—oh, boy! And on Friday, fish day, a fish loaf with macaroni and cheese or a Russian fish pie called perok, not to be forgotten. Dried fish was plentiful all winter.

14 LENA life story of my mother

DISEASES

In the early 1930s, diseases hit Alaska. They included diphtheria, whooping cough, measles and scarlet fever. Two of our brothers came down with scarlet fever. There was only one doctor at the Bethel Hospital. People were dying off since the doctor couldn't get around to treat all the sick, and there was not enough medication. Our aunt Bessie contracted tuberculosis and died, leaving a daughter, Ruby, and a son, Wilfred. Ruby moved in with us, becoming another sister, while the grandparents took Wilfred. In his early life, he was taken by diphtheria. There were communications sent by radio to the government teachers and health workers who received medication, to use it to treat those that needed it the most.

When scarlet fever hit our home, we had an old doctor on the other side. Our home was quarantined with large skull and crossbones signs on both the back and front doors. My brothers had a room of their own and the rest of us had to stay away from school and couldn't associate with the rest of the village. It seemed forever until we were able to go anywhere. The boys were very sick but came out of it okay, except for heart murmurs. They had to take special medications for a long time. By the time they were inducted into the service they were fine and must have outgrown the fault.

16   LENA life story of my mother

Akiak. Our home at left and Grandparent's Joe Venes house.

Diphtheria hit at the same time as the whooping cough, in spring of 1940. With the whooping cough, so many babies seemed to have had it. We lost our baby brother, Amel, and our neighbors, the Clement Saras, lost theirs, too. What a sad time it was! Mom was the only grown person who got diphtheria and was so sick that we almost lost her, too. The doctor was so busy, trying to save people. After a long time, Mom finally got well.

Then the measles came. I can still remember how we had to stay in a dark room for many, many days. The whole village was down, and the older ones tried in all ways to help each other. As we lay in our beds with blankets over the bedroom windows, an airplane flew over. I was the one that had to peek to see who it was. I was about eleven years old, and to this day I have worn glasses.

The plane was bringing Willie Chaney home with his new bride, Pauline. My father and his were so happy that they came. The two became our nursemaids, running up and down stairs with water and juices since everyone else was sick in bed.

One day Pauline took over and Willie went down and chopped some ice and made a large batch of ice cream. We were all feverish and what a wonderful thing that was! It seems we all got better after they came.

One year we all wound up with the seven-year itch. We had to be treated with some strong sulfa-type salve. All the students came down with it. It took a while to get over that, and thank goodness it didn't last for seven years!

Once in awhile, someone from the reindeer camp would come to the village and bring lice. When one got it the rest of the school was infested. When lice hit the village, we'd make sure to clean extra thoroughly, including washing underwear and heads more carefully than ever. It was such a hard time to get rid of that, too. Mom would go through our clothes, and require extra bathing, washing, and inspecting heads. She was so careful with us that although we were exposed, we never actually got lice ourselves. We would get a charge out of the native helpers when they were inspecting heads on some of the other kids though—when they found a louse they would take it between their thumb and fingernails and crack them dead. We could even hear them pop! Just the thought of that still gives us the shivers! When we had such a time with all the problems and everyone got well, the bad times were soon forgotten.

We didn't know too much about cancer until Joe Chaney developed a sore on his mouth where he held the pipe that he smoked. He left for Anchorage and then went out to Mayo Clinic in Minnesota. When he returned, the doctors thought that it had been contained but a year later it came back again. I can remember how sick he was, and that he stayed in the Bethel hospital until he passed away.

Then our Uncle Wilfred Reno came down with the same thing. He had married after losing Aunt Bessie, and he and his second wife had three children. The youngest, Charles, was about eight months. Reno was very ill when he was sent to the Anchorage hospital, and he knew he wasn't coming back home again. He made the arrangements with our folks to take Charlie and raise him, since his wife wasn't well either. So Charlie was adopted by us. The two older ones were sent to the Catholic Holy Cross mission, both passing away at the Mission at an early age.

The Missions served a useful purpose for Mother in a certain way. The Chaney boys were always full of stories about how a person was treated at the Mission schools. When disobedient, a student had to work extra hard and sometimes go to bed early without any dinner. When we were naughty, Mom threatened to send us to send us to Holy Cross or to the Moravian Mission at Kwethluk. We laugh about that now, but when we were kids, the thought was terribly frightening!

CLOTHES

A steamship from Seattle came up to Bethel on the Kuskokwim River twice during the summer, once in early spring and again in the fall. It would bring supplies for the trading posts and local orders for individuals. Merchandise ordered from Seattle was anything for building, and food. From Sears, Roebuck and Co. we'd get radios, clothes or sewing material. Staples included flour, sugar, canned vegetables and fruit, dried fruits and beans, eggs, butter in brine inside wooden kegs, and corned beef. We also ordered dried milk called Klim, powdered juice we had to mix in pitchers for use, canned meat including Spam and ham, and shortening and oils for cooking.

Sternwheelers, the Tana or the Northwestern, would meet the ships in Bethel to unload for villages up and down the Kuskokwim. There were other privately-owned scows that also did lightering.

Flour was sent in bags, and after filling the flour bins, Mom would bleach the sacks out and use the material for making clothes, dishtowels, curtains and nice underclothes for panties, slips, or nightgowns. When she made underslips, she'd crochet nice neck pieces and lower lace that looked so pretty. Yarn that came, we had to roll into balls as they always came in skeins. It was the kids' job to do that. Our father always made a race out of it. It was usually an evening job besides our school work. I can never remember any store-bought socks, hats, mittens, or caps. Mom was constantly knitting. She was such a hard worker, preparing meals, cleaning and sewing all the time.

With washable cotton material, dresses and kuspuks were made. The kuspuks are a dress-shaped knee-length outerwear used by most all Alaskans, and are still popular. They are used as a windbreaker made with a hood and wrist bands, for doing outside work. They were a protection from mosquitoes. We would draw the face tie close to the face since we didn't have mosquito dope in those days, and it was a great help when we had to weed gardens and do outside work in the summer.

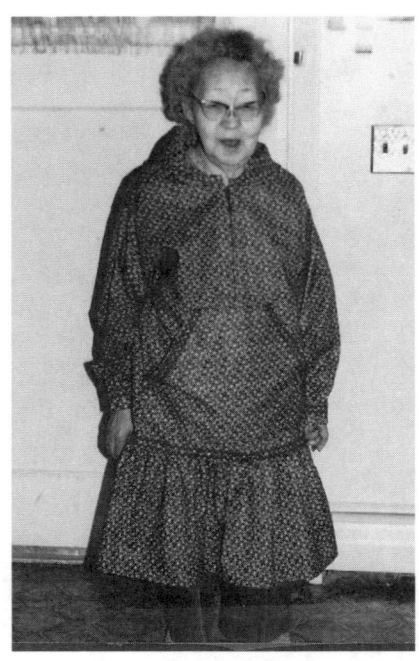

Mom in her Kuspuk.

In the home, Mom made bed nets of cheesecloth as protection from mosquitoes, draped over each bed for a good night's sleep. Buhach, a powder substance, was burned in the homes when the mosquitoes got too bad. Repellant for the bugs came to Bethel when the army troops came. It was awfully strong and burned the skin but it really worked.

Weeding the gardens, as we had so many, was quite a chore. Our father made smudge pots from old empty gas cans, and he burned green grass in them around the perimeter of the garden as we weeded. It helped to keep the mosquitoes away. Kuspuks were made for the men, hunters, woodcutters or whoever else had to work outside. The men's kuspuks were fur parkies with the fur against the skin and cotton material on the outside. The cotton kuspuks were always made of washable-type heavy material. The men wore their kuspuks a little below the waist.

Hair Kits - Kaapaaqs, Sewing Kits - Kakiviks, Russian Beads, Ivory Tobacco Holder - Iqmik, Eskimo Knife - Ulu.

Winter wear. All Fur Coat and Mukluks. Papa, Momma and Hanna.

There were so many of us small children that it was a big job to keep us warm. Village adults would donate old outgrown coats or winter items to our folks, which Mom made over. We were always happy to get a new jacket or coat. They were made so warm for outdoor play or work.

Mother made a certain type of sewing kit called a "kakivik", pronounced "gu-gee-wik". She had several that she used for her own projects, and made some as gifts for special people. This kit was made from a sturdy piece of fabric, usually wide-wale corduroy, and was shaped as a rectangle approximately 10 X 14 inches— some larger, some smaller. The kakivik had many pocketed sections sewn into the front, and the back was left plain. Hers in particular held scissors, thread, needles, (large curved ones, plus regular fabric needles, and the three-cornered type for skinsewing), buttons, a round flat piece of beeswax, (for coating thread when sewing skins), and other emergency items. Each pocketed section as well as the entire kakivik had contrasting binding around it, and on top of the binding she sewed a simple beaded design in straight running stitches. One end of the kakivik angled outward in a shallow "v" shape. Inside the point of that "v", there was a special pocket that held her thimbles. She used either a metal thimble or one made from the skin of the "oogruk", which is a bearded seal. The oogruk thimble was very thin, hard, and fit over the tip and pad of the finger. It was held in place by a band across the fingernail. At the outside point of the kakivik, there dangled an 8" length of binding that was about 3/8" wide. At the end of that binding were always knotted a few large Russian trade beads. When not in use, the kakivik was rolled up from the straight end first, all the pockets to the inside, leaving the dangling piece to be wrapped around the roll to secure it closed. This fine sewing kit that Mom handmade was given only to those closest to her heart.

Parkies and mukluks and mittens were made from muskrat, tundra squirrels, rabbit, and reindeer skin. The prettiest parkies were made for women of squirrel, with borders, tassels, and hoods of wolf and wolverine. The men had shorter parkies made with reindeer hide or muskrat skins, and they were heavier. Babies had mostly rabbit skin. Mukluks were worn during the winter months but we always seemed to have shoepaks for warmer weather. Mother sewed and designed each item along with the help of her Eskimo helpers.

Mom sewed her Squirrel Skin Coat.

We have always associated the smell of roses with our mother. She especially loved them and was a great fan of the Avon "Roses, Roses" products. Her children and grandchildren all remember that when we opened the door to her bedroom, we were treated with that lovely scent.

Mom had the habit of chewing a leaf-type tobacco that most Eskimos used. Their word for it was "iq'mik". She had so many nice, small decorative containers for iq'mik given to her as gifts through the years. She also made and used beautiful, beaded hairnets called kaapaaqs that all the married women used to distinguish them from the single women. When she died in 1992, we each received an iq'mik container or a kaapaaq as a souvenir to remind us of our mother.

5 generations! (left to right) Mom, granddaughter Renee, great-granddaughter Sherene, daughter Sis and great-great-grandson Joshua.

24 LENA life story of my mother

FISHING

After the ice went out in the early spring, it was time to worry about the fish coming in late May or the first part of June. The smelts were the first fish. We took our tents, boats and dipnets and moved about five miles below Akiak to a place called "the smelting slough", and camped out in our tents for about three days. We had to net these small fish in scoops as they came. We'd dip with pole nets, and had tubs to fill with fish. The days were long and everyone had their turn at dipping. An accident happened when one of the younger children fell in the slough and an older one pulled him out. There were others camping at the same place, so between our turns dipping, we all had fun visiting and game-playing. The older ones made a commitment to look out better for the younger ones. When our boat was full and the smelts had all gone by, we cleared camp and piled into the boat, started the Johnson gas motor, and headed for home.

In the days to come, it was so busy! My mother and the boys went out in the woods and got a lot of small pond willows, which were tied at the ends for stringing the smelts on and hanging on racks to dry. It was the girls' job to do the stringing. Now that wasn't an easy job with our kuspuks, leaning over a bin holding the smelts. Sometimes it took us a couple long days to finish them. The boys came along and hauled the strung smelts in a wheelbarrow to hang on the racks. Used for dog food, some were also dried and smoked in the smoke house and were good for eating. We hated this smelt job as it was so smelly and all the washing never seemed to get the odor out.

Early spring smelt rack and part of our dog team.

When the king salmon started running, Mom got really busy. Salmon made up a great deal of our wintertime diet, and Mother was terribly particular about how our "eating fish" was prepared.

Nobody was allowed to go near those kings but her. She got her "ulu" sharpened up and ready to go. The ulu is an Eskimo knife that is made in a crescent shape and kept very sharp. It can outperform most modern knives. Nowadays it is made from cutting a round tablesaw blade in thirds. The teeth are ground off, leaving a fine cutting edge. At the top of the ulu, where the center of the saw blade once was, a bone or ivory handle is attached and it is made to fit the grasp of the user very nicely. They are efficient knives and the native users are really dextrous with those blades.

Mother shooed us all away while she performed her art. She would behead, gut, and fillet those kings in

King Salmon cut and prepared for drying by Mother.

no time flat. She would then either slice across the fish, making 3/4" cuts which would allow the fish to dry faster in slabs, or strip them lengthwise, either way right through the tail so they could hand easily on the poles. They were brined in a certain way, hung, then smoked with alder brush until properly dried for eating. We kids were only allowed to handle the smaller salmon, the silvers or reds, since they were not as important and were often used for dog feed in the winter.

Brined and cut fish in smoke house by Mom.

The ulus have caught on as a peculiar gift for tourists to take home to their friends and relatives after a vacation to Alaska. There are many commercial varieties now, most cheaply made and with gaudy artwork on the blades and handles. In any case, they are still often used for skinning animals, cutting through frozen meat, slicing vegetables, chopping anything you could possibly wish to—and believe it or not, they slice pizzas wonderfully!

When the other smaller fish came we did the fish-cutting by the river, where the husky dogs were tied. We'd have a fire going to make dog feed for the dogs, and hanging rack to dry the fish for them too. The reds and silver salmon were salted in barrels for the winter, and we did a lot of canning and jarring. We had no refrigeration so had to take care of the fish right away. The days were long, so after work we would get together with the village kids and have a ball game, marbles, horseshoes, or croquet. If it was a nice day we would go up the beach to our favorite swimming hole.

GREEN THUMB

Mother loved flowers. All the years we were being raised, the house had so many plants, including fuchsias, geraniums and ivies. I can remember our father complaining about the light being blocked out by the plants, but we all knew he liked plants also. One cold winter evening, the boys went to the other side of the river for a dance. I don't recall why we girls couldn't go—maybe we were being punished for something or another. The boys came home late and left the living room door open by mistake. When the folks woke up the next morning, the flowers were all frozen. Oh, how mad Mom got! Of course, no one would admit who was the culprit. Papa sympathized with her and got after the boys for not closing the door right. Later he confessed to us girls with a sheepish grin, "Now we can see out of the windows!" By spring and summer the plants were grown back again in the windows, and more were blooming along the outside of the house.

The wildflowers outdoors were abundant also. One day we kids went outside to pick flowers and find frogs. We all came home so happy with our catch. I was wearing a summer straw hat, and when we got home, I called Mom and greeted her by lifting my hat—and out jumped a frog. I didn't know that she was deathly afraid of frogs. She almost fell over, and yelled at me to get that thing out, right now! It startled her so much that I knew I should never do that to her again.

Mom in her home at Bethel.

ESKIMO DANCES

In the early days, each village had a big Eskimo dance, held in a large community round sod house, called a gusgik. There was one large hut in each village where meetings were held, and a spot right in the middle of it, where a fire was built for "qaasiq", which is steambaths, or for potlatches. The main Eskimo dance of the year was held there. Invited friends and guests from other villages came and they enjoyed a potlatch. The burning pit was underground, with a large hole on the top for smoke to go out of when a fire was burned. The hole was a fresh-air vent otherwise. Benches were set up around the middle for seating, and the men did the drumming with round walrus skin drums and they beat on them as they sang. The songs were stories made up to show what was done in their lives, like hunting birds, trapping, seal and walrus hunting, or anything else. The women did most of the dancing with lovely fur parkies, and each held a dance fan made from basket-woven coastal grasses, a reindeer beard, feathers, and colored beads. They did their dance in tune with the beating of the drums. Once in awhile a man would come out and he'd dance on his knees. Good dancers of the village included Mrs. Eddie Owens, Mrs. Egoak, the Jacksons, Waskas, Kawagleys, and one happy lady we all called Rosie Woman because she had such rosy cheeks. Some had names that were used like Lame Jimmy, One-Eyed Paul, and even Fat Maggie.

Anyway, a good time was had by all, and a large potlatch was served at the end and it was held for three or four days. Then about those years, the missionaries put a stop to the dances and speaking Eskimo in schools, because it was claimed to be heathen. Those ideas were proven wrong, and dances are back again. Not much more could be done for speaking, because they did it anyway.

Joe Williams had a store on the other side with a pool hall, and he showed silent movies on the weekends. Usually they were cowboy movies or old comedies. It was entertaining for everyone, especially when Sarah Percy would operate the player piano, pumping away on the pedals.

CHRISTMAS

With Christmas coming each year, preparations were begun in November. Fruit cakes were made and stored away, nuts shelled since we got a sack of mixed nuts, and they were chopped and made ready for cookies, fudge, and cakes. Mom had so many good recipes that we all still use. The folks and most everyone in the village made homebrew while we kids made root beer. We bottled it and put it away since pop was so expensive to get. A Christmas spruce tree was cut down by the boys and set up. Most all decorations were made by us. We strung popcorn, and last of all we put on the candles, real candles with a clipping for the tree. We lit them and watched so closely, in case of fire. There were two gifts for each of us, usually something we really needed in clothing, and a toy. Someone would make a trip to Bethel by dogsled to get oranges and apples and Christmas candy.

Most dances were held in our home, as it was the largest. The tree was placed on the treadle sewing machine, and village instruments were played. The large, hand-wind record player was used. I can remember everyone dancing to a fast schottische, and over went the Christmas tree! Mom was yelling and everyone running to the rescue, replacing all the trimmings and lights. Thank goodness the candles weren't lit. It was all put back in place and the dance was continued. If the phonograph needed winding and got slow, someone would break their dance and rush over to wind the handle on the machine. A good time was always had by all.

I got an unusual gift on my birthday and at Christmas. In villages, the custom is that when a close friend dies, a newborn child is given the name of the deceased. I was one named Agoovak, and I'd receive nice gifts from her family. Sometimes they would be nice mukluks, scarves, or mittens, but this particular Christmas I got a tanned black bear skin presented to me. We had so much fun with that, especially scaring our young brother Charlie and other little children with it. Mom put a stop to that by having the skin cut up for a nice pair of mukluks for me. Today the practice of naming a newborn after a deceased person is still customary in villages.

GAMES

After our school homework, the neighbor kids would come over to our home. We had a round dining table, and we'd all sit around and play cards and games, including five hundred rummy, canasta, pinochile, chinese checkers, or Monopoly. Sometimes the folks would join us for games. It was so funny as it delighted my father to beat Mom. When she'd lose she'd get so mad and threaten not to play again, but the next time she was ready to play, and it made her happy to win. The evening would go fast until Papa, out of the game, would start to make wood shavings to start the morning fire. We all knew it was time to go to bed. Wherever we played we got the signal from the fathers of the house.

Saturday nights was bath night. The huge copper kettle was warmed up and from the smallest to the oldest, we took our turns bathing. It took a lot of water as there were several changes.

Sunday was a special day of rest. We could go for dog team rides or visit another village. We could also go to the Moravian Church on the other side of the river unless we had a visiting Catholic father on our side. Sometimes we'd go to a neighbor's that played the piano, and we'd sing religious songs. Other times, we'd go sledding or play games. One of us girls would be elected to bake a cake or cookies as dessert for a good dinner that was always prepared on Sunday. Our father made homemade skates, just like Hans Brinker skates, and skis. It seemed we had lots of snow, so we'd build snow tunnels and igloos. We'd slide down the hill with our large basket sled, halfway across the river just to do it again and again without tiring.

Since there were no airplanes in those days, the Catholic priest would come with a large dog team to stay for awhile. My Grandpa Joe Venes had a bunkhouse where the Father stayed, and the miners from New York Alaska Gold Mining Co. (called Nyac) came and spent the winter. The men would go back to the mine in early spring for their work. They would take the older boys to work if the boys were out of school, then at freezeup in the fall they all came home again. Anyway, the Catholic Father was great entertainment at our school, with stories and singing. Mass was held at our home as we had the largest family, and Mom made meals for him. He came from Holy Cross on the Yukon. He would travel back up the Kuskokwim on to the Yukon River and back to Holy Cross. They also had other priests traveling around the coast.

There were also the Moravian missionaries that settled in Bethel. They too traveled to the villages, with big dog teams in winter, or during the summer, in gas boats.

LAPLANDERS

The first Laplanders that came from Norway were hired by the government to come with their families to teach the Eskimos how to herd and take care of reindeer. There were four groups in Alaska, at Nome, Unalakleet, Bristol Bay, and the Kuskokwim. The Kuskokwim group lived in our village. There were four Lapp families, and some of the men found women in Alaska to marry. Their children went to our school with us. They built homes for their families, and had their herds about a hundred miles from Akiak toward the Alaska Range foothills where they could graze them. At that time we had no beef, and the moose and caribou did not come into our area, so the reindeer was our main source of meat. Most of the Laplanders were the families of the four Sara brothers, Mike, Peter, Clement, and Morten, the latter having died shortly after arriving in Alaska. Their sister, Ellen, became the wife of Jens Kvamme. There were also Lars Nelson, Perr Spain, Ole Polk, and a little brother and sister pair called Karen and Ante. Their sister Kristine was married to Pete Sara. Some of them could not speak English. They all wore their fancy turned-up boots made of reindeer hide and had red decorations on them. The men kept their families at Akiak and would come to check on them, while they worked their field of reindeer. My grandfather had built a large one-room territorial school house in the middle of Akiak where we all went to school.

I can remember Karen so well. She was such a small person, about four feet five inches, the same as her little brother Ante. She would like to come to the house to visit Mom, as Mom treated her to tea and some delicacies. We could always hear her coming and warn Mom. Mom had a certain chair for her to sit in. Since Karen couldn't speak English, it was hard to visit. After she had her treat, she'd sit for awhile and spit on the floor. Of course we kids would all giggle as we knew Mom disliked that. Karen would then wipe it by smearing it around with her Lapp boots. Mom would try to explain to her about not doing that, even placing an empty can by her chair, but when she came again she'd repeat her habit. We quit laughing after Karen left, as the one that laughed the hardest had to get the Clorox bottle and start cleaning.

The Lapps always had plenty of reindeer meat brought in from the herds. They'd build large racks off the ground and would cut up their supplies for drying in the early spring, then when dry they would store the meat away for their food supply. What they didn't know was that we kids would raid their dried meat. They never seemed to realize what feasts we had with it. We were never caught having our picnics. It was so good!

There was one little Laplander by the name of Ole Polk. He was the youngest, and he'd tease and cause fights with the village boys. We'd all pester him and egg him on. He lived toward the back of the village and it was a ways to go. He'd come down to get a load of water from the river with two buckets and a shoulder yoke. We'd watch for him, and when he'd stop for a rest someone would run out to pester him. He'd chase them to get even, and someone else would turn his water buckets over. So it took most all day for him to make one trip. Other aggravating things were done to him to get him mad so we could have fun. He must have enjoyed the problems, because when we didn't see him for awhile, he'd come looking for the kids.

40   LENA life story of my mother

BURBOT OR LUSH

There was hardly any fresh fish in the winter, so my father and the boys built a large fish trap, cut a hole in the river ice, and set it out to catch lush. All the villagers were catching fish that was under the ice. The trap was checked each day while the run was on. Some days hardly any were caught and other days a lot. When there was a good catch, they were given to the villagers who wanted some. Everyone wanted fresh fish, and they were delicious. Lush have a big liver that was such a delicacy. They are a very ugly fish but were a treat for everyone, including the heads. Mother cleaned and prepared the fish for dinners, baked or boiled. She usually had the head for herself. We girls in our early teens always wanted one, but she didn't cook us any as there were so many bones to watch out for.

One day there were a lot in the trap. All the village got a good feed. Mom cooked up some and decided to give us girls a treat. Dinner was being served on the round dining room table. She had ladled four enormous heads to cool until we came to the table. Just as we were about to sit down, there came a knock on the door and our father let in our Norwegian neighbor, Mr. Ole Anderson. We girls left the room in a hurry as we were so embarrassed about the big fish heads. After a brief chat with Papa, Mr. Anderson said, "Well, I'd best go home, as my wife is waiting on me for supper." Then, with amusement, he added, "So your girls can come to the table to eat their heads." It was a good laugh for them both. Norwegians are also fish-lovers, and they no doubt were having the same dinner at their homes. It didn't take us long to make it to the table to enjoy our fish heads.

THE WAR

When the war broke out and Japan raided Pearl Harbor and the Aleutian Islands, everything was so restrictive. Darkness was advised in all the villages. We put heavy blankets over the windows, and all the older ones listened to news on their Sears, Roebuck radios. Army planes brought troops to Bethel and stationed them there and McGrath, as well as other places around Alaska as needed. Our grown boys that were of service age were my brothers Sonny and Butch; uncles Joe Jr. and Elias Venes; Adam and Jack Kawagley; the Kvamme boys, Albert and Jimmy; Middy and Joe Chaney; and Patrick Smith. They all left to serve their country. We girls of the village, Hanna, Ruby, Aunt Nora, Catherine and Alice Kawagley, all got married and left Akiak. A few of us not of marriageable age stayed home. Our folks, our grandmother Annun, a few elders, and the Laplanders were left. A few years later the rest of us found our men and got married, leaving home as well.

In 1945 when the war was declared over, the boys started coming home. The news came that the army transport with our brother, Sonny, and his troops aboard, had plunged into the Bay of India and all were lost. He had been stationed in Italy. Our mother was so devastated at his loss. We did our best to console her. We all came back home, Hanna and I with our children, (our husbands still serving their time in the military), and Bessie, Cutie, Butch, and Charlie. The plane was never salvaged, and the only sign of the tragedy was debris in the water. It was such a sorrowful loss for all of us.

Our husbands were discharged from the service, and we moved to Bethel. We spent a lot of time with our folks. Bessie and Cutie got married and left, and our brothers went to work. Charlie became a pilot. Hanna's son Glenn and my daughter Rene'e spent a lot of time with their grandparents, Mom and Papa, at Akiak.

Sonny and Charlie Laraux

After the war, the school at Akiak had to be closed. People were moving away. Willie and Pauline Chaney moved to Nyac along with our uncle Joe Venes Jr., where another territorial school opened up. Hanna and I lived in Bethel where Charlie came and stayed with us to finish elementary school. One winter I stayed at Akiak with the folks until my husband returned from the service. I taught Charlie home-school with a Calvert correspondence course. For his high school years, our folks sent him to the Holy Cross mission. Then he went on to Fairbanks, where he later took up flying for Wien. From there he moved on to Delta Airlines and stayed with them until his retirement in 2000.

The older folks passed away, including my grandfather and the Laplanders. The younger generation married, moving away pair-by-pair from Akiak. The storekeepers and miners left also, moving to the Lower 48 or on to other villages.

Our aunt Nora had met and married Charlie Guinn while she was still in her teens. She finished high school in Eklutna and Mt. Edgecumbe after her marriage. She went to college part-time at the University of Alaska in Fairbanks, including correspondence courses, while raising a family. She became a magistrate in Bethel, and later, the first Eskimo judge in the State of Alaska.

**Aunt Nora (Venes) Guinn
- First Eskimo judge in Alaska.**

(left to right) Annie Laraux, Charles, Aunt Nora, Sister Hanna, Mom and Butch.

46 LENA life story of my mother

LATER YEARS

In 1959 we lost our father to a stroke, leaving Mom alone. The family made so many trips to Akiak before that, but now Mom didn't spend too much time there since she was alone. My brother Butch had married Marilyn and they had a barging business in Bethel. In March of 1970, he decided to move Mom down to Bethel too. His sons, with my oldest, Robert, and our uncles, Elias and Joe, drove a tractor over the frozen Kuskokwim River to Akiak. There, they lifted the house off the foundation, put it on skids, and moved it fifty miles down the river, placing it next door to Butch's house. Mother was as happy as could be since her house was set down in a wide-open spot on the tundra where the blueberry and cranberry picking was good. We didn't have it that way in Akiak, being in the middle of all the trees, so now anyone passing by would see her picking berries to her heart's content outside of her own house. She could made her akutaq as often as she wanted! Her house remains on that spot to this day.

In the 1960s, I lived with my family out on Dimond Boulevard in Anchorage, before the Dimond Mall days.

Moving Mom's home to Bethel - 1970.

Moving Mom's house from Akiak to Bethel by Butch (down the river) 50 miles.

It seemed so far out of town then. Mother came to visit us and spent a while with us after visiting my sister Hanna and her family in Girdwood.

On afternoon my husband, Roy, and I decided to go to the closest grocery store, the Safeway on Northern Lights Boulevard. We left the kids home, and Grandma was having a nap. Bruce was in his teens then, and was working on his motorcycle. When we finally got home, Grandma was gone so I asked Bruce where Grandma was. This was his story: "Grandma woke up after you left and she decided she wanted to go see Charlie (her son who lived five miles away on Arctic Boulevard). Since there were no cars at home, she asked me to give her a ride on my motorcycle. I asked her if she was sure she wanted to go! 'Oh, come on, let's go!' she replied, so she jumped on behind me. We took off with her kuspuk and 'pelatook' (head scarf) blowing in the wind and Grandma screaming all the way to Charlie's house. We must have been a sight, people were stopping to see what all the commotion was about!" They made it okay, but she never asked Bruce to take her on a ride again. Bruce complained that his ribs were sore afterward from Grandma hanging on so hard, for dear life no doubt!

While visiting our sister Cutie in Tanana in 1975, Glenn

LENA life story of my mother   49

In Tanana - The Gregory Girls and Mom. Look-Alikes.

delivered Mom to a friend's house one winter day for an afternoon visit. She stepped out from behind the truck and a snow machine driver didn't see her in time and she was hit. She got a broken hip and lay in the hospital, recovering for a time before being released to go home. It was very serious, although she healed quickly. She was always an active person, but that's when she started going downhill. She was in her early seventies then. Her greatest fear was winding up in a rest home, which she always reminded us not to do to her. She said the patients there were too old for her and "half-nuts", her favorite expression.

Setting up house by Butch's in Bethel.

In the early summer of 1980, our brother Butch was working on his barge, welding a fuel tank. The tank exploded, killing him instantly. It was such grievous time for Mother, losing a third son. The next summer, Butch's son, called Deek, was welding a fuel tank for his truck when he had the very same thing occur, causing his death as well. Some years later, Butch's son Alfred would be killed while working heavy equipment on his property. It seems Mom and Marilyn shared so many of the same sorrows.

Mom spent the summers at her place in Bethel, where we would visit her, and the winters taking turns visiting us girls who had homes and children all over. Our brother,

Charlie, a captain for Delta, flew between the Lower 48 and Alaska. He would take Mother to visit our sister, Bess, and her family in Wichita Falls, Texas, Ruby in Moose Lake, Minnesota, his own family in Enumclaw, Washington, Lena in Fairbanks and Tanana, me in Wasilla, and Hanna in Girdwood and Clam Gulch. Delta's crew enjoyed Mother so much, and she got to be very well known among them. They fussed over her and waited on her, heart and soul.

Mom's last birthday party.
L-R Bess, Sis, Mom, Cutie, Hanna

Mom also spent time with my daughter Rene'e and her family in Anchorage. Rene'e entertained her a lot and did much to help her. Rene'e took Mother to Bingo, because she loved to go even if she could only play one card. She had the patience which I didn't. The caller would call a number, and Mom would say the number again and again until she found it on her card. One evening I came into the hall looking for them. I said, "Hi, Mom, how you doing?" She replied, "Oh, not so good, I guess. I'm trying to win, as hard as I could." She did win one time, believe it or not, all by herself. She was so happy! She and Rene'e went out and bought her an Alaska gold nugget watch that she had been longing for.

EILEEN JENKINS

Keep on the Sunny side

Eileen Jenkins - Mother's half-sister.

Carrie Anvil - Mom's half-sister.

A few years after losing our Dimond house to a fire, my husband and I had a farm prior to the pipeline days in the middle of Wasilla, Alaska. We had chickens, pigs, ducks, geese, and a calf we called Henry. Mom liked to come and visit us. She enjoyed the animals and the fresh eggs. The last time Mom came, the calf had gotten quite big.

One day, Mom and I had gone to the grocery store. We returned with our arms full of groceries. She started up the back porch, four or five steps. She was so small that she was on all fours, crawling up slowly. Henry had been getting feisty, and we hadn't noticed that he was coming toward us. I thought he was going to knock me over and I started running toward Mom and the stairs. She saw the calf, too, heading our way. I ran past her as she was climbing, and I said to her, "Hurry up, Mom, it's coming, get out of the way!" Of course, Henry stopped, and Mom got in the house and sat on a chair. She was bawling me out and laughing at the same time. She said, "And you were going to let me get killed!" Such a big laugh we had. I had to explain to her that all I thought about was that Henry would knock us down, he was coming so fast.

Not only was Mother always active in keeping her own home clean, she would always do work at our houses too when she came to visit. She couldn't stay idle for long. She would wash dishes by standing on cans of vegetables so she could reach the sink. Besides all her hard work, she would "relax" by knitting up a storm for the next Christmas, or play five hundred rummy with whoever would challenge her. Even though we had to read all the directions to her and count out the money, Mom would beat us time after time playing Monopoly. She would always buy up every property she could and never, ever sell or make deals.

Large Family Wedding - Mother, 2nd in row 2.

When my son Roy Jr. married Julane in Wasilla, what a good time we all had. Mom was staying with Rene'e then. A nice church wedding was followed by a reception at the VFW with drinks and lots of good food. Champagne was passed around and Mom had a few. When someone filled the glasses, she'd say, "T'ank you, I just loves that shom-peen!" When it was time to go home, Rene'e rounded up all her children and Mom to take them home to Anchorage. Mother sat with the kids in the back seat. All the way home the kids were yelling, and Rene'e wanted to know what was going on back there. The kids said, "It's Grandma, she's so mad at us having to leave the party, she keeps pinching all of us!" Rene'e laughed and said, "It's a good thing we came home when we did!"

Mom often taught her children and grandchildren how important it is to be kind to others, especially those in need. She had the firm belief that if a person were generous to others, he would always be taken care of by others in his old age—her version of the saying that "What goes around comes around." While raising her family, we noted how thoughtful she was to her dear Eskimo friends on the other side of the river who

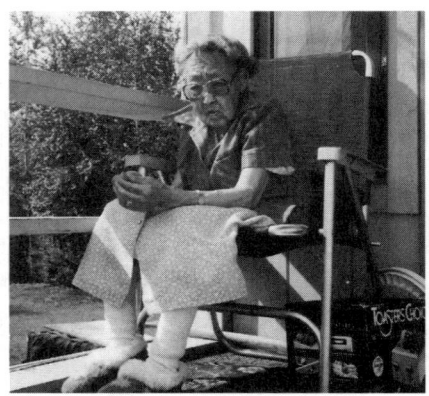

Mom enjoying the sun porch at the Gregory's.

were not as well off. They were the ones who received our outgrown clothing and gifts of food. She herself was the proof that her philosophy is true—in Mother's old age, she had many friends and relatives tending to her every need, traveling long distances to visit with her, always loaded with gifts of native foods, wild game, and finery to wear or display. All the people who knew her were very attentive to her.

(left to right) Bess, Butch, Cutie, Sis, Mom and Ruby.

Mom had her favorite expressions that she would use on us. If we did or said something that upset her, she would say, "You be good now, you know I'm your mother and I been born you." She even said this to her adopted children. We called them "her famous last words", and don't think they were limited to our childhood—she gave us this speech even when she was in her latter years!

Three years before she passed away, Mom moved up to Fairbanks to stay with our youngest sister Lena full-time. That was her baby girl and they were close. She spent quite a bit of time with them before that in Tanana, where they owned a trading post and flying service. She liked it there in Fairbanks, a comfortable, quiet home with nice gardens and flowers. She would sit for hours in the summer admiring the view from the porch when the bugs weren't too bad. She had a lot of visitors from around Alaska. Everyone loved her and she was always so happy to see her old friends.

Mother was particularly proud of her descendants. At any family gathering, she would study the crowd and quietly announce, "And just t'ink—all these people came from me!" She often asked her grandchildren to take notes as she counted out the numbers of grandchildren and great-grandchildren she had at the time, add them up, and tell her the total. We always considered the

Mom in her home at Bethel.

living, dead, and adopted in those numbers. Today, the fall of 2002, they total nine children, forty-two grandchildren, and one hundred twenty-five great-grandchildren—and, as Mother would say, "that's not counting the 'uccidents'!"

Mother died at the age of 90 while living with Cutie and Glenn in Fairbanks. Her wish was granted; she had a nice place to enjoy in her later years instead of in the forgotten rest home which she called "the crazy house". On the night of November 25, 1992, she wasn't feeling too well. She lay down, went to sleep, and went on to heaven.

We had a beautiful funeral for her in Anchorage and another enormous service in Bethel. There was a wonderful group of native gospel singers that sang for her, including "The Lord's Prayer" in Eskimo, called "Atamta". In Bethel the singers included her half-sisters, Carrie Anvil and Eileen Jenkins, and Eileen's daughter Ina. Mom's body was flown out to Bethel, and the men in our family and circle of friends took it out by snow machine to Old Akiak and hand-dug her grave in the family plot. It was a terribly stormy day, and none of us women were allowed to fly out there to attend the burial because of the dangerous weather conditions. We had bid our mother tua-i-ngunrituq, which means "This isn't the end; we'll meet again", before her body was taken out to Akiak. We were consoled that she had had such a peaceful death and remained mentally sharp and quite physically able until her passing. Every summer our relatives visit the family grave site, tidying it up and placing fresh flowers there.

Mom and her best friend, Elizabeth Cornelius.

5 generations! (left to right) Great-great-grandson Ethan, great-granddaughter Christy, daughter Sis, Mom and granddaughter Aimee.

LENA life story of my mother

THE LORD'S PRAYER
(Yup'ik)

ATAMTA

A-tam-ta qil-iit
qain-at-nel-nuq
tam-aa-ten tut-naur-tuq
at-ren el-pet

Tam-aa-ten piu-naur-tuq
pi-cir-kiu-cin
nu-nam qain-a-ni
qil-iit-qain-at-ni-lu-ci-mi-tun

Neq-ka-mek nuu-qek-nam-ten-nek
ci-kir-kut er-ner-pak
ca-li pell-ug-cet-la-qi-ki
as-ill-nu-put wan-ku-ta

Pellug-cet-lau-cim-cetun
ca-na-yug-cet-aar-tem-tenek

As-iil-nir-ceten-na-qu-ma-lem-teni
as iil-nir-ceten-na-qu-ma-lem-teni

Taug-aam av-ius-kut
iq-lum tun-ii-nek

A—men, a—men, a—men.

58 LENA life story of my mother